GOD'S
SOVEREIGNTY
IN THE
SALVATION
OF MEN

GREAT CHRISTIAN BOOKS
LINDENHURST, NEW YORK

GOD'S SOVEREIGNTY
IN THE
SALVATION
OF MEN

JONATHAN EDWARDS

A GREAT CHRISTIAN BOOKS publication
Great Christian Books is an imprint of Rotolo Media
160 37th Street Lindenhurst, New York 11757
(631) 956-0998
www.GreatChristianBooks.com
email: mail@greatchristianbooks.com

God's Sovereignty in the Salvation of Men
ISBN 978-1-61010-050-2 Paperback

Jonathan, Edwards, 1703–1758
God's Sovereignty in the Salvation of Men / by Jonathan Edwards
     p.   cm.
A "A Great Christian Book" book
GREAT CHRISTIAN BOOKS an imprint of Rotolo Media
ISBN 978-1-61010-050-2
Recommended Dewey Decimal Classification: 234
Suggested Subject Headings:
1. Religion—Christian literature—Soteriology
2. Christianity—The Bible—The Gospel
I. Title

The book and cover design for this title are by Michael Rotolo (www.michaelrotolo.com). It is typeset in the Minion typeface by Adobe Inc. and is quality manufactured in the great United States on premium, archival quality acid-free paper stock. To discuss the publication of your Christian manuscript or out-of-print book, please contact Great Christian Books. www.greatchristianbooks.com

God's Sovereignty in the Salvation of Men

Extracted From
Seventeen Occasional Sermons—Sermon IV

CONTENTS

INTRODUCTION

"Therefore hath he mercy on whom he will have mercy, and whom he will he hardeneth."

—Romans 9:18

THE apostle, in the beginning of this chapter, expresses his great concern and sorrow of heart for the nation of the Jews, who were rejected of God. This leads him to observe the difference which God made by election between some of the Jews and others, and between the bulk of that people and the Christian Gentiles. In speaking of this he enters into a more minute discussion of the sovereignty of God in electing some to eternal life, and rejecting others, than is found in any other part of the Bible; in the course of which he quotes several passages from the Old Testament, confirming and illustrating this doctrine. In the ninth verse he refers us to what God said to Abraham, showing his election of Isaac before Ishmael—"For this is the word of promise; At this time will I come, and Sarah shall have a son:" then to what God had said to Rebecca, showing his election of Jacob before Esau; "The elder shall serve the younger:" in the thirteenth verse, to a passage from Malachi, "Jacob have I loved, but Esau have I hated:" in the fifteenth verse, to what God said to Moses, "I will have mercy on whom I will have mercy; and I will have compassion on whom I will have compassion:" and the verse preceding the text, to what God says to Pharaoh, "For the scripture saith unto Pharaoh, Even for this same purpose have I raised thee up, that I might show my power in thee, and that my name might be declared throughout all the earth." In what the apostle says in the text, he seems to have respect especially to the two last-cited passages: to what God said to Moses in the fifteenth verse, and to what he said to Pharaoh in the verse immediately preceding. God said to Moses, "I will have mercy on whom I will have mercy." To this the apostle refers in the former part of the text. And we know how often it is said of Pharaoh, that God hardened his heart. And to this the apostle seems to have respect in the latter part of the text; "and whom he will he hardeneth." We may observe in the text,—

1. God's different dealing with men. He hath mercy on some, and hardeneth others. When God is here spoken of as hardening some of the children

of men, it is not to be understood that God by any positive efficiency hardens any man's heart. There is no positive act in God, as though he put forth any power to harden the heart. To suppose any such thing would be to make God the immediate author of sin. God is said to harden men in two ways: by withholding the powerful influences of his Spirit, without which their hearts will remain hardened, and grow harder and harder; in this sense he hardens them, as he leaves them to hardness. And again, by ordering those things in his providence which, through the abuse of their corruption, become the occasion of their hardening. Thus God sends his word and ordinances to men which, by their abuse, prove an occasion of their hardening. So the apostle said, that he was unto some "a savor of death unto death." So God is represented as sending Isaiah on this errand, to make the hearts of the people fat, and to make their ears heavy, and to shut their eyes; lest they should see with their eyes, and hear with their ears, and understand with their heart, and convert, and be healed. Isa. 6:10. Isaiah's preaching was, in itself, of a contrary tendency, to make them better. But their abuse of it rendered it an occasion of their hardening. As God is here said to harden men, so he is said to put a lying spirit in the mouth of the false prophets. 2 Chron. 18:22. That is, he suffered a lying spirit to enter into them. And thus he is said to have bid Shimei curse David. 2 Sam. 16:10. Not that he properly commanded him; for it is contrary to God's commands. God expressly forbids cursing the ruler of the people. Exod. 22:28. But he suffered corruption at that time so to work in Shimei, and ordered that occasion of stirring it up, as a manifestation of his displeasure against David.

2. The foundation of his different dealing with mankind; viz. his sovereign will and pleasure. *"He hath mercy on whom he will have mercy, and whom he will he hardeneth."* This does not imply, merely, that God never shows mercy or denies it against his will, or that he is always willing to do it when he does it. A willing subject or servant, when he obeys his lord's commands, may never do any thing against his will, nothing but what he can do cheerfully and with delight; and yet he cannot be said to do what he wills in the sense of the text. But the expression implies that it is God's mere will and sovereign pleasure, which supremely orders this affair. It is the divine will without restraint, or constraint, or obligation.

Doctrine: God exercises his sovereignty in the eternal salvation of men.

He not only is sovereign, and has a sovereign right to dispose and order in that affair; and he not only might proceed in a sovereign way, if he would, and nobody could charge him with exceeding his right; but he actually does so; he exercises the right which he has. In the following discourse, I propose to show,

I. WHAT IS GOD'S SOVEREIGNTY,

II. WHAT GOD'S SOVEREIGNTY IN THE SALVATION OF MEN IMPLIES,

III. THAT GOD ACTUALLY DOTH EXERCISE HIS SOVEREIGNTY IN THIS MATTER,

IV. THE REASONS FOR THIS EXERCISE.

ONE

WHAT IS GOD'S SOVEREIGNTY?

The sovereignty of God is his absolute, independent right of disposing of all creatures according to his own pleasure. I will consider this definition by the parts of it.

The will of God is called his mere pleasure,

1. In opposition to any constraint. Men may do things voluntarily, and yet there may be a degree of constraint. A man may be said to do a thing voluntarily, that is, he himself does it; and, all things considered, he may choose to do it; yet he may do it out of fear, and the thing in itself considered be irksome to him, and sorely against his inclination. When men do things thus, they cannot be said to do them according to their mere pleasure.

2. In opposition to its being under the will of another. A servant may fulfil his master's commands, and may do it willingly, and cheerfully,

and may delight to do his master's will; yet when he does so, he does not do it of his own mere pleasure. The saints do the will of God freely. They choose to do it; it is their meat and drink. Yet they do not do it of their mere pleasure and arbitrary will; because their will is under the direction of a superior will.

3. In opposition to any proper obligation. A man may do a thing which he is obliged to do, very freely; but he cannot be said to act from his own mere will and pleasure. He who acts from his own mere pleasure, is at full liberty; but he who is under any proper obligation, is not at liberty, but is bound. Now the sovereignty of God supposes, that he has a right to dispose of all his creatures according to his mere pleasure in the sense explained. And his right is absolute and independent. Men may have a right to dispose of some things according to their pleasure. But their right is not absolute and unlimited. Men may be said to have a right to dispose of their own goods as they please. But their right is not absolute; is has limits and bounds. They have a right to dispose of their own goods as they please, provided they do not do it contrary to the law of the state to which they are subject, or contrary to the law of God. Men's right to dispose of their things as they will, is not absolute, because it is not independent. They have not an independent right to what they have, but in some things depend on the community to which they belong, for the right they have; and in everything depend on God. They receive all

the right they have to anything from God. But the sovereignty of God imports that he has an absolute, and unlimited, and independent right of disposing of his creatures as he will.

TWO

WHAT DOES GOD'S SOVEREIGNTY IN THE SALVATION OF MEN IMPLY?

In answer to this inquiry, I observe, it implies that God can either bestow salvation on any of the children of men, or refuse it, without any prejudice to the glory of any of his attributes, except where he has been pleased to declare, that he will or will not bestow it. It cannot be said absolutely, as the case now stands, that God can, without any prejudice to the honour of any of his attributes, bestow salvation on any of the children of men, or refuse it; because, concerning some, God has been pleased to declare either that he will or that he will not bestow salvation on them; and thus to bind himself by his own promise. And concerning some he has been pleased to declare, that he never will bestow salvation upon them; viz. those who have committed the sin against the Holy Ghost. Hence, as the case now stands, he is obliged; he cannot bestow salvation in one case, or refuse it in the other, without prejudice to the honour of his truth. But God exercised his sovereignty in making these declarations. God was not obliged to promise that he would save all who believe in Christ; nor was he obliged to declare, that he who committed the sin against the Holy Ghost should never be forgiven. But it pleased him so to declare. And had it not been so that God had been pleased to oblige himself in these cases, he might still have either bestowed salvation, or refused it, without prejudice to any of his attributes. If it would in itself be prejudicial to any of his attributes to bestow or refuse salvation, then God would not in that matter act as absolutely sovereign. Because it then ceases to be a merely arbitrary thing. It ceases to be a matter of absolute liberty, and is become a matter of necessity or obligation. For God cannot do any thing to the prejudice of any of his attributes, or contrary to what is in itself excellent and glorious. Therefore,

I. God can, without prejudice to the glory of any of his attributes, bestow salvation on any of the children of men, except on those who have committed the sin against the Holy Ghost. The case was thus when man fell, and before God revealed his eternal purpose and plan for redeeming men by Jesus Christ. It was probably looked upon by the angels as a thing utterly inconsistent with God's attributes to save any of the children of men. It was utterly inconsistent with the honour of the divine attributes to save any one of the fallen children of men, as they were in themselves. It could not have been done had not God contrived a way consistent with the honour of his holiness, majesty, justice, and truth. But since God in the gospel has revealed that nothing is too hard for him to do, nothing beyond the reach of his power, and wisdom, and sufficiency; and since Christ has wrought out the work of redemption, and fulfilled the law by obeying, there is none of mankind whom he may not save without any prejudice to any of his attributes, excepting those who have committed the sin against the Holy Ghost. And those he might have saved without going contrary to any of his attributes, had he not been pleased to declare that he would not. It was not because he could not have saved them consistently with his justice, and consistently with his law, or because his attribute of mercy was not great enough, or the blood of Christ not sufficient to cleanse from that sin. But it has pleased him for wise reasons to declare that that sin shall never be forgiven in this world, or in the world to come. And so now it is contrary to God's truth to save such. But otherwise there is no sinner, let him be ever so great, but God can save him without prejudice to any attribute; if he has been a murderer, adulterer, or perjurer, or idolater, or blasphemer, God may save him if he pleases, and in no respect injure his glory. Though persons have sinned long, have been obstinate, have committed heinous sins a thousand times, even till they have grown old in sin, and have sinned under great aggravations: let the aggravations be what they may; if they have sinned under ever so great light; if they have been backsliders, and have sinned against ever so numerous and solemn warnings and strivings of the Spirit, and mercies of his common providence: though the danger of such is much greater than of other sinners, yet God can save them if he pleases, for the sake of Christ, without any prejudice to any of his attributes. He may have mercy on whom he will have mercy. He may have mercy on the greatest of sinners, if he pleases, and the glory of none of his attributes will be in the least sullied. Such is the sufficiency of the satisfaction and righteousness of Christ, that none of the divine attributes stand in the way of the salvation of any of them. Thus the glory of any attribute did not at all suffer by Christ's saving some of his crucifiers.

1. God may save any of them without prejudice to the honour of his holiness. God is an infinitely holy being. The heavens are not pure in his sight. He is of purer eyes than to behold evil, and cannot look on iniquity. And if God should in any way countenance sin, and should not give proper testimonies of his hatred of it, and displeasure at it, it would be a prejudice to the honour of his holiness. But God can save the greatest sinner without giving the least countenance to sin. If he saves one, who for a long time has stood out under the calls of the gospel, and has sinned under dreadful aggravations; if he saves one who, against light, has been a pirate or blasphemer, he may do it without giving any countenance to their wickedness; because his abhorrence

of it and displeasure against it have been already sufficiently manifested in the sufferings of Christ. It was a sufficient testimony of God's abhorrence against even the greatest wickedness, that Christ, the eternal Son of God, died for it. Nothing can show God's infinite abhorrence of any wickedness more than this. If the wicked man himself should be thrust into hell, and should endure the most extreme torments which are ever suffered there, it would not be a greater manifestation of God's abhorrence of it, than the sufferings of the Son of God for it.

2. God may save any of the children of men without prejudice to the honour of his majesty. If men have affronted God, and that ever so much, if they have cast ever so much contempt on his authority; yet God can save them, if he pleases, and the honour of his majesty not suffer in the least. If God should save those who have affronted him, without satisfaction, the honour of his majesty would suffer. For when contempt is cast upon infinite majesty, its honour suffers, and the contempt leaves an obscurity upon the honour of the divine majesty, if the injury is not repaired. But the sufferings of Christ do fully repair the injury. Let the contempt be ever so great, yet if so honourable a person as Christ undertakes to be a Mediator for the offender, and in the mediation suffer in his stead, it fully repairs the injury done to the majesty of heaven by the greatest sinner.

3. God may save any sinner whatsoever consistently with his justice. The justice of God requires the punishment of sin. God is the Supreme Judge of the world, and he is to judge the world according to the rules of justice. It is not the part of a judge to show favour to the person judged; but he is to determine according to a rule of justice without departing to the right hand or left. God does not show mercy as a judge, but as a sovereign. And therefore when mercy sought the salvation of sinners, the inquiry was how to make the exercise of the mercy of God as a sovereign, and of his strict justice as a judge, agree together. And this is done by the sufferings of Christ, in which sin is punished fully, and justice answered. Christ suffered enough for the punishment of the sins of the greatest sinner that ever lived. So that God, when he judges, may act according to a rule of strict justice, and yet acquit the sinner, if he be in Christ. Justice cannot require any more for any man's sins, than those sufferings of one of the persons in the Trinity, which Christ suffered. Rom. 3:25,26. "Whom God hath set forth to be a propitiation through faith in his blood; to declare his righteousness, that he might be just, and the justifier of him which believeth in Christ."

4. God can save any sinner whatsoever, without any prejudice to the honour of his truth. God passed his word, that sin should be punished with death, which is to be understood not only of the first, but of the second death. God can save the

greatest sinner consistently with his truth in this threatening. For sin is punished in the sufferings of Christ, inasmuch as he is our surety, and so is legally the same person, and sustained our guilt, and in his sufferings bore our punishment. It may be objected, that God said, If thou eatest, thou shalt die; as though the same person that sinned must suffer; and therefore why does not God's truth oblige him to that? I answer, that the word then was not intended to be restrained to him, that in his own person sinned. Adam probably understood that his posterity were included, whether they sinned in their own person or not. If they sinned in Adam, their surety, those words, "if thou eatest," meant, if thou eatest in thyself, or in thy surety. And therefore, the latter words, "thou shalt die," do also fairly allow of such a construction as, thou shalt die in thyself, or in thy surety. Isa. 42:21. "The Lord is well pleased for his righteousness" sake, he will magnify the law and make it honourable." But,

II. God may refuse salvation to any sinner whatsoever, without prejudice to the honour of any of his attributes.

There is no person whatever in a natural condition, upon whom God may not refuse to bestow salvation without prejudice to any part of his glory. Let a natural person be wise or unwise, of a good or ill natural temper, of mean or honourable parentage, whether born of wicked or godly parents;

let him be a moral or immoral person, whatever good he may have done, however religious he has been, how many prayers soever he has made, and whatever pains he has taken that he may be saved; whatever concern and distress he may have for fear he shall be damned; or whatever circumstances he may be in; God can deny him salvation without the least disparagement to any of his perfections. His glory will not in any instance be the least obscured by it.

1. God may deny salvation to any natural person without any injury to the honour of his righteousness. If he does so, there is no injustice nor unfairness in it. There is no natural man living, let his case be what it will, but God may deny him salvation, and cast him down to hell, and yet not be chargeable with the least unrighteous or unfair dealing in any respect whatsoever. This is evident, because they all have deserved hell: and it is no injustice for a proper judge to inflict on any man what he deserves. And as he has deserved condemnation, so he has never done any thing to remove the liability, or to atone for the sin. He never has done any thing whereby he has laid any obligations on God not to punish him as he deserved.

2. God may deny salvation to any unconverted person whatever without any prejudice to the honour of his goodness. Sinners are sometimes ready to flatter themselves, that though it may not be contrary to the justice of God to condemn them,

yet it will not consist with the glory of his mercy. They think it will be dishonorable to God's mercy to cast them into hell, and have no pity or compassion upon them. They think it will be very hard and severe, and not becoming a God of infinite grace and tender compassion. But God can deny salvation to any natural person without any disparagement to his mercy and goodness. That, which is not contrary to God's justice, is not contrary to his mercy. If damnation be justice, then mercy may choose its own object. They mistake the nature of the mercy of God, who think that it is an attribute, which, in some cases, is contrary to justice. Nay, God's mercy is illustrated by it, as in the twenty-third verse of the context. "That he might make known the riches of his glory on the vessels of mercy, which he had afore prepared unto glory."

3. It is in no way prejudicial to the honour of God's faithfulness. For God has in no way obliged himself to any natural man by his word to bestow salvation upon him. Men in a natural condition are not the children of promise; but lie open to the curse of the law, which would not be the case if they had any promise to lay hold of

THREE

GOD DOES ACTUALLY EXERCISE HIS SOVEREIGNTY IN MEN'S SALVATION

We shall show how he exercises this right in several particulars.

1. In calling one people or nation, and giving them the means of grace, and leaving others without them. According to the divine appointment, salvation is bestowed in connexion with the means of grace. God may sometimes make use of very unlikely means, and bestow salvation on men who are under very great disadvantages; but he does not bestow grace wholly without any means. But God exercises his sovereignty in bestowing those means. All mankind are by nature in like circumstances towards God. Yet God greatly distinguishes some from others by the means and advantages which he bestows upon them. The savages, who live in the remote parts of this continent, and are under the

grossest heathenish darkness, as well as the inhabitants of Africa, are naturally in exactly similar circumstances towards God with us in this land. They are no more alienated or estranged from God in their natures than we; and God has no more to charge them with. And yet what a vast difference has God made between us and them! In this he has exercised his sovereignty. He did this of old, when he chose but one people, to make them his covenant people, and to give them the means of grace, and left all others, and gave them over to heathenish darkness and the tyranny of the devil, to perish from generation to generation for many hundreds of years. The earth in that time was peopled with many great and mighty nations. There were the Egyptians, a people famed for their wisdom. There were also the Assyrians and Chaldeans, who were great, and wise, and powerful nations. There were the Persians, who by their strength and policy subdued a great part of the world. There were the renowned nations of the Greeks and Romans, who were famed over the whole world for their excellent civil governments, for their wisdom and skill in the arts of peace and war, and who by their military prowess in their turns subdued and reigned over the world. Those were rejected. God did not choose them for his people, but left them for many ages under gross heathenish darkness, to perish for lack of vision; and chose one only people, the posterity of Jacob, to be his own people, and to give them the means of grace. Ps. 147:19,20. "He showeth his word unto Jacob, his statutes and his judgments unto Israel. He hath not dealt so with any nation; and as for his judgments, they have not known them." This nation were a small, inconsiderable people in comparison with many other people. Deut. 7:7. "The Lord did not set his love upon you, nor choose you, because ye were more in number than any people; for ye were the fewest of all people." So neither was it for their righteousness; for they had no more of that than other people. Deut. 9:6. "Understand therefore, that the Lord thy God giveth thee not this good land to possess it for thy righteousness; for thou art a stiff-necked people." God gives them to understand, that it was from no other cause but his free electing love, that he chose them to be his people. That reason is given why God loved them; it was because he loved them. Deut. 7:8. Which is as much as to say, it was agreeable to his sovereign pleasure, to set his love upon you.

God also showed his sovereignty in choosing that people, when other nations were rejected, who came of the same progenitors. Thus the children of Isaac were chosen, when the posterity of Ishmael and other sons of Abraham were rejected. So the children of Jacob were chosen, when the posterity of Esau were rejected: as the apostle observes in the seventh verse, "Neither because they are the seed of Abraham, are they all children; but in Isaac shall thy seed be called": and again in verses 10, 11, 12, 13. "And not only this; but when Rebekah also had conceived by one, even by our father Isaac; the children moreover being not yet born, neither having done any good or evil, that the promise of God according to election might stand, not of works, but of him that calleth; it was said unto her, The elder shall serve the younger. As it is written, Jacob have I loved, but Esau have I hated." The apostle has not respect merely to the election of the persons of Isaac and Jacob before Ishmael and Esau; but of their posterity. In the passage, already quoted from Malachi, God has respect to the nations, which were the posterity of Esau and Jacob; Mal. 1:2,3. "I have loved you, saith the Lord. Yet ye say, Wherein hast thou loved us? Was not Esau Jacob's brother? saith the Lord: yet I loved Jacob; and I hated Esau, and laid his mountains and his heritage waste for the dragons of the wilderness." God showed his sovereignty, when Christ came, in rejecting the Jews, and calling the Gentiles. God rejected that nation who were the children of Abraham according to the flesh, and had been his peculiar people for so many ages, and who alone possessed the one true God, and chose idolatrous heathen before them, and called them to be his people. When the Messiah came, who was born of their nation, and whom they so much expected, he rejected them. He came to his own, and his own received him not. John 1:11. When the glorious dispensation of the gospel came, God passed by the Jews, and called those who had been heathens, to enjoy the privileges of it. They were broken off, that the Gentiles might be grafted on. Rom. 11:17. She is now called beloved, that was not beloved. And more are the children of the desolate, than the children of the married wife. Isa. 54:1. The natural children of Abraham are rejected, and God raises up children to Abraham of stones. That nation, which was so honoured of God, have now been for many ages rejected, and remain dispersed all over the world, a remarkable monument of divine vengeance. And now God greatly distinguishes some Gentile nations from others, and all according to his sovereign pleasure.

2. God exercises his sovereignty in the advantages he bestows upon particular persons. All need salvation alike, and all are, naturally, alike undeserving of it; but he gives some vastly greater advantages for salvation than others. To some he assigns their place in pious and religious families, where they may be well instructed and educated, and have religious parents to dedicate them to God, and put up many prayers for them. God places some under a more powerful ministry than others, and in places where there are more of the outpourings of the Spirit of God. To some he gives much more of the strivings and the awakening influences of the Spirit, than to others. It is according to his mere sovereign pleasure.

3. God exercises his sovereignty in sometimes bestowing salvation upon the low and mean, and denying it to the wise and great. Christ in his sovereignty passes by the gates of princes and nobles, and

enters some cottage and dwells there, and has communion with its obscure inhabitants. God in his sovereignty withheld salvation from the rich man, who fared sumptuously every day, and bestowed it on poor Lazarus, who sat begging at his gate. God in this way pours contempt on princes, and on all their glittering splendor. So God sometimes passes by wise men, men of great understanding, learned and great scholars, and bestows salvation on others of weak understanding, who only comprehend some of the plainer parts of Scripture, and the fundamental principles of the Christian religion. Yea, there seem to be fewer great men called, than others. And God in ordering it thus manifests his sovereignty. 1 Cor. 1:26,27,28. "For ye see your calling, brethren, how that not many wise men after the flesh, not many mighty, not many noble, are called. But God hath chosen the foolish things of the world to confound the wise; and God hath chosen the weak things of the world to confound the things which are mighty; and base things of the world, and things which are despised, hath God chosen, yea, and things which are not, to bring to nought things that are.

4. In bestowing salvation on some who have had few advantages. God sometimes will bless weak means for producing astonishing effects, when more excellent means are not succeeded. God sometimes will withhold salvation from those who are the children of very pious parents, and bestow

it on others, who have been brought up in wicked families. Thus we read of a good Abijah in the family of Jeroboam, and of a godly Hezekiah, the son of wicked Ahaz, and of a godly Josiah, the son of a wicked Amon. But on the contrary, of a wicked Amnon and Absalom, the sons of holy David, and that vile Manasseh, the son a good Hezekiah. Sometimes some, who have had eminent means of grace, are rejected, and left to perish, and others, under far less advantages, are saved. Thus the scribes and Pharisees, who had so much light and knowledge of the Scriptures, were mostly rejected, and the poor ignorant publicans saved. The greater part of those, among whom Christ was much conversant, and who heard him preach, and saw him work miracles from day to day, were left; and the woman of Samaria was taken, and many other Samaritans at the same time, who only heard Christ preach, as he occasionally passed through their city. So the woman of Canaan was taken, who was not of the country of the Jews, and but once saw Jesus Christ. So the Jews, who had seen and heard Christ, and saw his miracles, and with whom the apostles laboured so much, were not saved. But the Gentiles, many of them, who, as it were, but transiently heard the glad tidings of salvation, embraced them, and were converted.

5. God exercises his sovereignty in calling some to salvation, who have been very heinously wicked, and leaving others, who have been moral and reli-

gious persons. The Pharisees were a very strict sect among the Jews. Their religion was extraordinary. Luke 18:11. They were not as other men, extortioners, unjust, or adulterers. There was their morality. They fasted twice a week, and gave tithes of all that they possessed. There was their religion. But yet they were mostly rejected, and the publicans, and harlots, and openly vicious sort of people, entered into the kingdom of God before them. Matt. 21:31. The apostle describes his righteousness while a Pharisee. Philip. 3:6. "Touching the righteousness which is of the law, blameless." The rich young man, who came kneeling to Christ, saying, Good Master, what shall I do, that I may have eternal life, was a moral person. When Christ bade him keep the commandments, he said, and in his own view with sincerity, "All these have I kept from my youth up." He had obviously been brought up in a good family, and was a youth of such amiable manners and correct deportment, that it is said, "Jesus beholding him, loved him." Still he was left; while the thief, that was crucified with Christ, was chosen and called, even on the cross. God sometimes shows his sovereignty by showing mercy to the chief of sinners, on those who have been murderers, and profaners, and blasphemers. And even when they are old, some are called at the eleventh hour. God sometimes shows the sovereignty of his grace by showing mercy to some, who have spent most of their lives in the service of Satan, and have little left to spend in the service of God.

6. In saving some of those who seek salvation, and not others. Some who seek salvation, as we know both from Scripture and observation, are soon converted; while others seek a long time, and do not obtain at last. God helps some over the mountains and difficulties which are in the way; he subdues Satan, and delivers them from his temptations: but others are ruined by the temptations with which they meet. Some are never thoroughly awakened; while to others God is pleased to give thorough convictions. Some are left to backsliding hearts; others God causes to hold out to the end. Some are brought off from a confidence in their own righteousness; others never get over that obstruction in their way, as long as they live. And some are converted and saved, who never had so great strivings as some who, notwithstanding, perish.

FOUR

WHY GOD DOES THUS EXERCISE HIS SOVEREIGNTY IN THE ETERNAL SALVATION OF THE CHILDREN OF MEN

1. It is agreeable to God's design in the creation of the universe to exercise every attribute, and thus to manifest the glory of each of them. God's design in the creation was to glorify himself, or to make a discovery of the essential glory of his nature. It was fit that infinite glory should shine forth; and it was God's original design to make a manifestation of his glory, as it is. Not that it was his design to manifest all his glory to the apprehension of creatures; for it is impossible that the minds of creatures should comprehend it. But it was his design to make a true manifestation of his glory, such as should represent every attribute. If God glorified one attribute, and not another, such manifestation of his glory would be defective; and the representation would not be complete. If all God's attributes are not manifested, the glory of none of them is manifested as

it is: for the divine attributes reflect glory on one another. Thus if God's wisdom be manifested, and not his holiness, the glory of his wisdom would not be manifested as it is; for one part of the glory of the attribute of divine wisdom is, that it is a holy wisdom. So if his holiness were manifested, and not his wisdom, the glory of his holiness would not be manifested as it is; for one thing which belongs to the glory of God's holiness is, that it is a wise holiness. So it is with respect to the attributes of mercy and justice. The glory of God's mercy does not appear as it is, unless it is manifested as a just mercy, or as a mercy consistent with justice. And so with respect to God's sovereignty, it reflects glory on all his other attributes. It is part of the glory of God's mercy, that it is sovereign mercy. So all the attributes of God reflect glory on one another. The glory of one attribute cannot be manifested, as it is, without the manifestation of another. One attribute is defective without another, and therefore the manifestation will be defective. Hence it was the will of God to manifest all his attributes. The declarative glory of God in Scripture is often called God's name, because it declares his nature. But if his name does not signify his nature as it is, or does not declare any attribute, it is not a true name. The sovereignty of God is one of his attributes, and a part of his glory. The glory of God eminently appears in his absolute sovereignty over all creatures, great and small. If the glory of a prince be his power and dominion, then the glory of God is his absolute sovereignty. Herein appear God's infinite greatness and highness above all creatures. Therefore it is the will of God to manifest his sovereignty. And his sovereignty, like his other attributes, is manifested in the exercises of it. He glorifies his power in the exercise of power. He glorifies his mercy in the exercise of mercy. So he glorifies his sovereignty in the exercise of sovereignty.

2. The more excellent the creature is over whom God is sovereign, and the greater the matter in which he so appears, the more glorious is his sovereignty. The sovereignty of God in his being sovereign over men, is more glorious than in his being sovereign over the inferior creatures. And his sovereignty over angels is yet more glorious that his sovereignty over men. For the nobler the creature is, still the greater and higher doth God appear in his sovereignty over it. It is a greater honour to a man to have dominion over men, that over beasts; and a still greater honour to have dominion over princes, nobles, and kings, than over ordinary men. So the glory of God's sovereignty appears in that he is sovereign over the souls of men, who are so noble and excellent creatures. God therefore will exercise his sovereignty over them. And the further the dominion of any one extends over another, the greater will be the honour. If a man has dominion over another only in some instances, he is not therein so much exalted, as in having absolute dominion over his life, and fortune, and all he has.

So God's sovereignty over men appears glorious, that it extends to every thing which concerns them. He may dispose of them with respect to all that concerns them, according to his own pleasure. His sovereignty appears glorious, that it reaches their most important affairs, even the eternal state and condition of the souls of men. Herein it appears that the sovereignty of God is without bounds or limits, in that it reaches to an affair of such infinite importance. God, therefore, as it is his design to manifest his own glory, will and does exercise his sovereignty towards men, over their souls and bodies, even in this most important matter of their eternal salvation. He has mercy on whom he will have mercy, and whom he will he hardens.

APPLICATION

1. Hence we learn how absolutely we are dependent on God in this great matter of the eternal salvation of our souls. We are dependent not only on his wisdom to contrive a way to accomplish it, and on his power to bring it to pass, but we are dependent on his mere will and pleasure in the affair. We depend on the sovereign will of God for every thing belonging to it, from the foundation to the top-stone. It was of the sovereign pleasure of God, that he contrived a way to save any of mankind, and gave us Jesus Christ, his only-begotten Son, to be our Redeemer. Why did he look on us, and send us a Saviour, and not the fallen angels? It was from the

sovereign pleasure of God. It was of his sovereign pleasure what means to appoint. His giving us the Bible, and the ordinances of religion, is of his sovereign grace. His giving those means to us rather than to others, his giving the awakening influences of his Spirit, and his bestowing saving grace, are all of his sovereign pleasure. When he says, "Let there be light in the soul of such an one," it is a word of infinite power and sovereign grace.

2. Let us with the greatest humility adore the awful and absolute sovereignty of God. As we have just shown, it is an eminent attribute of the Divine Being, that he is sovereign over such excellent beings as the souls of men, and that in every respect, even in that of their eternal salvation. The infinite greatness of God, and his exaltation above us, appears in nothing more, than in his sovereignty. It is spoken of in Scripture as a great part of his glory. Deut. 32:39. "See now that I, even I, am he, and there is no God with me. I kill, and I make alive; I wound, and I heal; neither is there any that can deliver out of my hand." Ps. 115:3. "Our God is in the heavens; he hath done whatsoever he pleased." Daniel 4:34,35. "Whose dominion is an everlasting dominion, and his kingdom is from generation to generation. And all the inhabitants of the earth are reputed as nothing; and he doeth according to his will in the armies of heaven, and among the inhabitants of the earth; and none can stay his hand, or say unto him, What doest thou?" Our Lord Jesus Christ praised

and glorified the Father for the exercise of his sovereignty in the salvation of men. Matt. 11:25,26. "I thank thee, Oh Father, Lord of heaven and earth, because thou hast hid these things from the wise and prudent, and hast revealed them unto babes. Even so, Father, for so it seemed good in thy sight." Let us therefore give God the glory of his sovereignty, as adoring him, whose sovereign will orders all things, beholding ourselves as nothing in comparison with him. Dominion and sovereignty require humble reverence and honour in the subject. The absolute, universal, and unlimited sovereignty of God requires, that we should adore him with all possible humility and reverence. It is impossible that we should go to excess in lowliness and reverence of that Being, who may dispose of us to all eternity, as he pleases.

3. Those who are in a state of salvation are to attribute it to sovereign grace alone, and to give all the praise to him, who maketh them to differ from others. Godliness is no cause for glorying, except it be in God. 1 Cor. 1:29,30,31. "That no flesh should glory in his presence. But of him are ye in Christ Jesus, who of God is made unto us wisdom, and righteousness, and sanctification, and redemption. That, according as it is written, He that glorieth, let him glory in the Lord." Such are not, by any means, in any degree to attribute their godliness, their safe and happy state and condition, to any natural difference between them and other men, or to any

strength or righteousness of their own. They have no reason to exalt themselves in the least degree; but God is the being whom they should exalt. They should exalt God the Father, who chose them in Christ, who set his love upon them, and gave them salvation, before they were born, and even before the world was. If they inquire, why God set his love on them, and chose them rather than others, if they think they can see any cause out of God, they are greatly mistaken. They should exalt God the Son, who bore their names on his heart, when he came into the world, and hung on the cross, and in whom alone they have righteousness and strength. They should exalt God the Holy Ghost, who of sovereign grace has called them out of darkness into marvellous light; who has by his own immediate and free operation, led them into an understanding of the evil and danger of sin, and brought them off from their own righteousness, and opened their eyes to discover the glory of God, and the wonderful riches of God in Jesus Christ, and has sanctified them, and made them new creatures. When they hear of the wickedness of others, or look upon vicious persons, they should think how wicked they once were, and how much they provoked God, and how they deserved for ever to be left by him to perish in sin, and that it is only sovereign grace which has made the difference. 1 Cor. 6:10. Many sorts of sinners are there enumerated; fornicators, idolaters, adulterers, effeminate, abusers of themselves with mankind. And then in the eleventh verse, the apostle tells them, "Such were some of you; but ye are washed, but ye are sanctified, but ye are justified, in the name of the Lord Jesus, and by the Spirit of our God." The people of God have the greater cause of thankfulness, more reason to love God, who hath bestowed such great and unspeakable mercy upon them of his mere sovereign pleasure.

4. Hence we learn what cause we have to admire the grace of God, that he should condescend to become bound to us by covenant; that he, who is naturally supreme in his dominion over us, who is our absolute proprietor, and may do with us as he pleases, and is under no obligation to us; that he should, as it were, relinquish his absolute freedom, and should cease to be merely sovereign in his dispensations towards believers, when once they have believed in Christ, and should, for their more abundant consolation, become bound. So that they can challenge salvation of this Sovereign; they can demand it through Christ, as a debt. And it would be prejudicial to the glory of God's attributes, to deny it to them; it would be contrary to his justice and faithfulness. What wonderful condescension is it in such a Being, thus to become bound to us, worms of the dust, for our consolation! He bound himself by his word, his promise. But he was not satisfied with that; but that we might have stronger consolation still, he hath bound himself by his oath. Heb. 6:13, etc. "For when God made promise to Abraham, because he could swear by no greater,

he sware by himself; saying, Surely blessing I will bless thee, and multiplying I will multiply thee. And so, after he had patiently endured, he obtained the promise. For men verily swear by the greater; and an oath for confirmation is to them an end of all strife. Wherein God, willing more abundantly to show unto the heirs of promise the immutability of his counsel, confirmed it by an oath; that by two immutable things, in which it was impossible for God to lie, we might have a strong consolation, who have fled for refuge to lay hold upon the hope set before us. Which hope we have as an anchor of the soul, both sure and steadfast, and which entereth into that within the veil; whither the forerunner is for us entered, even Jesus, made an high priest for ever after the order of Melchisedec."

Let us, therefore, labour to submit to the sovereignty of God. God insists, that his sovereignty be acknowledged by us, and that even in this great matter, a matter which so nearly and infinitely concerns us, as our own eternal salvation. This is the stumbling-block on which thousands fall and perish; and if we go on contending with God about his sovereignty, it will be our eternal ruin. It is absolutely necessary that we should submit to God, as our absolute sovereign, and the sovereign over our souls; as one who may have mercy on whom he will have mercy, and harden whom he will.

5. And lastly. We may make use of this doctrine to guard those who seek salvation from two

opposite extremes—presumption and discouragement. Do not presume upon the mercy of God, and so encourage yourself in sin. Many hear that God's mercy is infinite, and therefore think, that if they delay seeking salvation for the present, and seek it hereafter, that God will bestow his grace upon them. But consider, that though God's grace is sufficient, yet he is sovereign, and will use his own pleasure whether he will save you or not. If you put off salvation till hereafter, salvation will not be in your power. It will be as a sovereign God pleases, whether you shall obtain it or not. Seeing, therefore, that in this affair you are so absolutely dependent on God, it is best to follow his direction in seeking it, which is to hear his voice today: "Today if ye will hear his voice, harden not your heart." Beware also of discouragement. Take heed of despairing thoughts, because you are a great sinner, because you have persevered so long in sin, have backslidden, and resisted the Holy Ghost. Remember that, let your case be what it may, and you ever so great a sinner, if you have not committed the sin against the Holy Ghost, God can bestow mercy upon you without the least prejudice to the honor of his holiness, which you have offended, or to the honour of his majesty, which you have insulted, or of his justice, which you have made your enemy, or of his truth, or of any of his attributes. Let you be what sinner you may, God can, if he pleases, greatly glorify himself in your salvation.

ABOUT THE AUTHOR

Jonathan Edwards (October 5, 1703 – March 22, 1758) was a preacher, theologian, and missionary to Native Americans. Edwards is widely acknowledged to be America's most important and original philosophical theologian, and one of America's greatest intellectuals. Edwards's theological work is very broad in scope, but he is often associated with his defense of Reformed Theology, the metaphysics of theological determinism, and the Puritan heritage. Recent studies have emphasized how thoroughly Edwards grounded his life's work on conceptions of beauty, harmony, and ethical fittingness, and how central The Enlightenment was to his mindset.

Edwards played a critical role in shaping the First Great Awakening, and oversaw some of the first fires of revival in 1733-1735 at his church in Northampton, Massachusetts. Edwards's sermon *Sinners in the Hands of an Angry God*, is considered a classic of early American literature, which he delivered during another wave of revival in 1741, following George Whitefield's tour of the Thirteen Colonies. Edwards is widely known for his many books: *The End For Which God Created the World; The Life of David Brainerd*, which served to inspire thousands of missionaries throughout the nineteenth century; and *Religious Affections*, which many Reformed Evangelicals read even today. Edwards died from a smallpox inoculation shortly after beginning the presidency at the College of New Jersey (later to be named Princeton University), and was the grandfather of Aaron Burr.

THE MISSION OF GREAT CHRISTIAN BOOKS

The ministry of Great Christian Books was established to glorify The Lord Jesus Christ and to be used by Him to expand and edify the kingdom of God while we occupy and anticipate Christ's glorious return. Great Christian Books will seek to accomplish this mission by publishing Gospel literature which is biblically faithful, relevant, and practically applicable to many of the serious spiritual needs of mankind upon the beginning of this new millennium. To do so we will always seek to boldly incorporate the truths of Scripture, especially those which were largely articulated as a body of theology during the Protestant Reformation of the sixteenth century and ensuing years. We gladly join our voice in the proclamations of— Scripture Alone, Faith Alone, Grace Alone, Christ Alone, and God's Glory Alone!

Our ministry seeks the blessing of our God as we seek His face to both confirm and support our labors for Him. Our prayers for this work can be summarized by two verses from the Book of Psalms:

> *"...let the beauty of the LORD our God be upon us, And establish the work of our hands for us; Yes, establish the work of our hands." —Psalm 90:17*

> *"Not unto us, O LORD, not unto us, but to your name give glory." —Psalm 115:1*

Great Christian Books appreciates the financial support of anyone who shares our burden and vision for publishing literature which combines sound Bible doctrine and practical exhortation in an age when too few so-called "Christian" publications do the same. We thank you in advance for any assistance you can give us in our labors to fulfill this important mission. May God bless you.

For a catalog of other great
Christian books including
additional titles by
John Calvin
contact us in
any of the following ways:

write us at:
Great Christian Books
160 37th Street
Lindenhurst, NY 11757

call us at:
631. 956. 0998

find us online:
www.greatchristianbooks.com

email us at:
mail@greatchristianbooks.com

Printed by Amazon Italia Logistica S.r.l.
Torrazza Piemonte (TO), Italy

58303287R00032